SONGS OF TRIUMPH

*

By the Same Author

*

WHITE FIRE
SILVER IN THE SUN
FLAME IN THE WIND
MISS HUMPTY COMES TO TEA
LIGHT OF THE YEARS
THIS GOLDEN SUMMIT
THE RADIANT QUEST
SPLENDOR AHEAD
FACING THE STARS
SOME BRIGHTER DAWN
BETWEEN ETERNITIES
THE LIFTED LAMP
THE WIND-SWEPT HARP
SONGS FOR COURAGE
SONGS OF HOPE
SONGS OF FAITH
SONGS FOR COMFORT
THE CRYSTAL FOUNTAIN
APPLES OF GOLD
JOURNEY INTO DAWN

*

Songs of Triumph

By

Grace Noll Crowell

HARPER & BROTHERS PUBLISHERS
NEW YORK

SONGS OF TRIUMPH

Copyright © 1946, 1955, 1956, 1957, 1959
by Grace Noll Crowell

Printed in the United States of America

All rights in this book are reserved. No part of the book may be used or reproduced in any manner whatsoever without written permission except in the case of brief quotations embodied in critical articles and reviews. For information address Harper & Brothers, 49 East 33rd Street, New York 16, N. Y.

G-I

Library of Congress catalog card number: 59–10332

This book is dedicated to all those who, spiritually undefeated, live through their difficult days with faith and high courage.

¶ Credit is due the following publications for permission to reprint certain poems in this book:

Unity Publications
The War Cry (Central and Southern)
The Pilgrim Press (Church in the Home)
The Message Magazine
The Baptist Convention (South)
The David C. Cook Publishing Company
  (Adult Bible Class)
The Methodist Publishing Company
The Christian Herald
The American Baptist Publication Society

CONTENTS

Triumph	13
Roadmates	14
The Same White Christ	15
The Undefeated	16
The Shield of Faith	17
The Arsenals of Strength	18
The Eternal Miracle	19
The Lonely Grandeurs	20
White Splendors	21
I Believe	22
Values That Abide	23
The Lord Hath Triumphed Gloriously	24
Word to a Journeying Pilgrim	25
A Question	26
A Night of Stars	27
A Poet Questions the Master	28
The Angelus	29
By Devious Ways	31
Loyalty	32
Faith	33
I Shall Walk Upon the Hills	34
In Thy Hand	35
Prayer for a Wider Vision	36
In Quietness	37

THE IMPREGNABLE ROCK	38
IMMORTALITY	39
ALTAR WITHIN THE HEART	40
CHARIOTS OF FIRE	41
A UNIVERSAL LANGUAGE	42
A PRAYER FOR THE WAKING ONES	43
THE OLD SIMPLICITIES	44
BECAUSE OF HIS COMPASSION	45
SUMMER EVENING	46
PRECIOUS FRUIT	47
A HOLY CURIOSITY	48
PREFERENCE	49
I SHALL GO ON	50
OUT OF THE IVORY PALACES	51
HARK! ACROSS THE WORLD	52

SONGS OF TRIUMPH

*

Triumph

To him that overcometh will I give to eat of the tree of life, which is in the midst of the paradise of God.

REVELATION 2:7

TRIUMPH! there is music in the word,
A cry of joy when the clamoring tumults cease,
And over the weary ones who have waited long
There suddenly settles a deep and blessed peace:
A peace so needed after the days of strife.
We have God's Word to help us through any hour:
"To him that overcometh I will give
To eat of the tree of life . . . I will give power . . ."
And although the days be difficult and long
Through any time of stress, it is wise to wait
That promised power, that precious golden fruit
Of victory that will come though soon or late.

Roadmates

YOU who are my roadmates, you who go
  Along the way with me, I do not know,
Save as I know myself. You have the same
Deep feeling that is mine—the inner flame
Of love for beauty, and a great capacity
For pity and compassion when you see
Another's hurt. You surely have, as I,
Known grief and sorrow as the years pass by,
And happiness and joy that lift the heart.
You must, as I have, often gone apart
To be alone with pain that none could share.
You question me: "How can you know?" you say,
And I make answer: "It is clear as day.
We are alike, made in God's image, so
Though you be stranger to me, yet I know."

The Same White Christ

THE same white Christ with the same divine compassion
Still walks the roadways of the earth today.
We may not see his form, his face, but surely
It is he who moves beside us on the way.
It is his hand that lifts the heavy burdens,
It is his touch that heals our many ills,
It is his strength preventing us from falling
As we tread earth's valleys and its steep rough hills.
The same white Christ! Thank God for that blest sameness:
Unchanged, unaltered through the stress of time
And through a vast eternity. Without him
We would fail and falter on our upward climb.
But we have his love, we lean upon his strength,
And we cannot fail through any lifetime length.

The Undefeated

THESE are the valiant ones who face their days
With courage drawn from some deep inner
source
That stays them through the weary waiting hours
And keeps them steadfast and serene, a force
That eyes have never seen nor have ears heard;
But to the ones who heed Christ's counseling
It has a name, a luster all its own:
A radiance called "Faith," a priceless thing.

The Shield of Faith

HE who bears within his hand
The shining shield of faith may go
A conqueror down any land,
Though battles rage and fires glow,
And though the enemy's sly might
May strive to take him by surprise,
That shield will send the sun's own light
Reflecting back to blind his eyes.

The shield of faith! O Lord, dear Lord,
I would lay hold so firmly now
Upon the brightness of thy Word,
Upon the promises that thou
Wilt be my helmet, shield, and spear
Through any dark tumultuous war,
That day by day and year by year
I may be more than conqueror.

The Arsenals of Strength

UNSEEN by human eyes
　Are the arsenals of strength:
Whether it be a tree's root,
Its strong and reaching length,
Or in a flower's growth
Springing up from the sod—
These are the arsenals
Equipped by the hand of God.

Unseen by earthly eyes
Are the forces in man's heart,
Where courage dwells, and faith's
Hidden bright springs start,
Where hope lies rooted deep
Waiting the seed's quick swell—
This is man's inner strength,
This is God's arsenal.

The Eternal Miracle

THERE is a road that mankind will remember
As long as there are trails that lead away
Into the mist of some blue far horizon:
The road that led to Jericho the day
When Christ reached out and healed one sorely stricken.
"A miracle! A miracle!" we cry,
And yet no less a miracle are answers
To our urgent pleadings as he passes by.

Jesus of Nazareth still walks earthly roadways,
He still performs his miracles when we
Cry out in desperate need, and do his bidding.
Before our eyes that once were blind we see
Him move in our behalf, and are aware
Of the eternal miracle of answered prayer.

The Lonely Grandeurs

IN FOLLOWING the swift onrush of the throng
We lay waste our powers and we spend
Strength we sorely need to keep us strong
To the far journey's end.

We forget the quietude we need:
The lonely grandeur of a place apart
Where manna will be sent on which to feed
To stay the hungry heart.

There we can cultivate the golden grain
Of honesty, integrity, and truth
From the idle, waste-land ground that may have lain
Fallow from our youth.

There are the lonely grandeurs to be found
By all who seek a quiet place to pray.
From our own mountainside God's voice will sound
Clearly out today.

White Splendors

THESE are earth's white splendors—these are they
That lift the spirit as time passes by:
The first white light that heralds a new day,
The flickering wings of gulls against the sky,
White moonlight shimmering on a distant sea,
White roses through an evening wet with dew,
Unbroken snow in its tranquility,
The guiding light of stars a dark night through.

And deep within man's spirit, something more:
Unshaken faith that sheds a clear white light,
High hope that knocks forever at his door
And will not be denied—all these are white,
And holiness gleams white across earth's sod,
Revealing the splendor of the truths of God.

I Believe

I BELIEVE that life is everlasting,
That there are higher hills for us to climb
And smoother sunlit roads for us to travel
Beyond the ancient boundaries of time.

I believe that love will last forever
If it be proven true upon the earth,
That somehow in a longer vast tomorrow
We can evaluate its precious worth.

I believe that faith will grow and strengthen
As we ascend beyond the farthest height,
That hope which sometimes here may fade and falter
Will burn there its undimmed and lifted light.

I believe that God, who is preparing
His children for new splendors, will be wise
To lead us softly that the sudden glory
Will not bewilder unaccustomed eyes.

Values That Abide

MERCY, kindness, justice—these abide
 Within the heart where God abides and are
The values that outlive the sun and moon,
And that outshine the brightest silver star.
A mind that dwells on purity and truth
Shares something of God's own clear thinking mind.
The heart that takes quick fire at the thought
Of sharing with the Holy One will find
Vast undiscovered reaches, inward powers,
New roads that hitherto have not been trod.
He will walk among the stars, his will attuned
To the beautiful clean mind and heart of God.
Values that abide—my soul, cling fast
To the eternal verities that last!

The Lord Hath Triumphed Gloriously
(EXODUS 15:21)

"SING ye to the Lord
   For he hath triumphed gloriously."
The ancient song still sounds
Across the lengthening years.
Always he has triumphed,
Always he will triumph—
O mankind, cease your doubting
And loose your hold on fears.

"Sing ye to the Lord."
Oh, may our praise arising
Be like the smoke of incense
Or like music upward flown;
Always he has triumphed,
Always he will triumph—
His is the greatest triumph
That ever has been known.

Word to a Journeying Pilgrim

STILL your hurrying heart, O journeying pilgrim,
Forging ahead beneath a burdening load.
You often may be weary, worn, and restless,
And feel there is no ending to the road;
But there are wayside pools by which to rest you,
And there is shade from many a greening tree.
There will be cold spring water for your thirsting
And glorious vistas for your eyes to see.

No doubt the journey's ending will be better
Than at the dawn or in the noontime heat.
Take heart. Look up—the hills ahead are golden;
The climb will be made easy for your feet.
And there upon the highest crest the sunset
Will point the way ahead with fingered flame,
And looking backward on the crimsoned lowlands
You will note the road was bright by which you came.

A Question

WHY should I long for other lands?
　　Why should I care to roam?
I can find the same skies over me,
The same green hills at home,
The same old earth beneath my feet,
The same moon sheds its light
Above my roof as that which floods
The Appian Way tonight.

The wild flowers down my country road
Yield perfume quite as sweet
As the costliest attars—why should I
Have restless hands and feet,
When the humanity surrounding me,
Of which I am a part,
Differs so very little from
The old-world folk at heart?

A Night of Stars

THERE is an ache within my heart for peace—
The world's voice joins me like an echoing cry,
My four walls close me far too closely in,
My roof shuts out the sky.
And so I turn and shut my door and go
Into the night, away from the hindering bars,
And standing there face-skyward, I am washed
By the rain of silver stars.

And I am cleansed and quieted; they move
With one accord upon their radiant quest.
So silent and assured they take their way,
My heart has found its rest.
There is an unseen power guiding them;
Because of his might not one has failed—I see
God back of the stars, he holds them in his hand,
And he holds me.

A Poet Questions the Master

"How shall I write?" I questioned the Lord of life:
"I would gather the ribbons of beauty in my hands
And fashion a poem till the page be rife
With color and light. I would travel to far-off lands
And write of the glories of which I have only heard:
Of mosques and temples, of the islands of the sea—
I would search the earth for some shining beautiful word
To describe a poet's strange wild ecstasy."

And lo, the Master made answer: "Write," he said,
"Write with your hands and your mind, but before you start
Your pen down an unmarred snowy page, be led
By my spirit—then, child, write with your heart.
Dip your pen in this fount, and you may say
What the troubled world is hungering for today."

The Angelus

OH, THAT a clear-struck bell might sound at evening
Over our land as it did in other lands,
When men and women would pause awhile to listen,
And stand with their heads bowed and with folded hands,
Thanking their God for the will and the strength to labor
And for the rest ahead at the set of sun,
As over the village and the meadowlands came pealing
The insistent call to prayer when the day was done.

Surely we, too, down the streets of our clamoring cities
Could catch the echo of some far distant bell,
Could heed it for a brief remembering moment,
And could lift a prayer of praise . . . Oh, who can tell

How far would be the reach of that pause of reverence,
When stilled by a bell the world's wild din would cease;
And how many hearts, home-bound in the tangling traffic,
Might find in that moment a hitherto unknown peace?

By Devious Ways

WE COME to God by devious ways, indeed.
The church—how blest it is; but we can find
God in the humblest home if we but seek
Him there with open heart and earnest mind.
A quiet room may be a wayside shrine
For one bound on a far, eternal quest,
And he can be companioned on the way
As the Lord God comes to be his special guest.

There are the shut-ins who cannot attend
The service of the church, but God supplies
Food for their hunger, for within his Book
Is knowledge enough to make the dullest wise.
They may not hear the choir's lifting voice
But they can catch the music of the spheres
Where the singing psalmist bids their hearts rejoice
With his songs that have the power to quiet fears.

Loyalty

THIS is my prayer—this is the prayer I pray—
Not for fame or fortune do I ask,
But to go forward bravely, day by day,
Loyal to my vision and my task.
Christ is the vision—his white purity
Lights up the darkest pathway that I tread.
Ever his vital words companion me.
I keep my eyes upon his form ahead.

To this, the task that has been given me,
I would be faithful, serving at my best.
Though menial and humble it may be,
I shall strive through it to earn my peace, my rest.
I would be loyal ever to the One
Who someday may cry out to me: "Well done!"

Faith

"WHEN Jesus saw their faith," the splendor came
Like blinding light, and the troubled, halt, and lame
Leapt with joy and shouted out his name.

Their load that had been burdensome was gone,
And the daylight broke for them like summer dawn
As gratefully and gladly they moved on.

So will our faith today, if it be bright,
Bring his ready answer, and the light
Will break with sudden glory on our sight.

His arm has not been shortened. Let us cling
To that immortal truth, remembering
That he has promised us "some better thing."

All that he asks is faith, and he will see
Its shining light, and lo, miraculously
Will come the blessing, friends, for you and me.

I Shall Walk Upon the Hills

I SHALL go out today
From my roof and my door,
I shall not carry my burdens along
As I have before;
I shall forget the carking cares,
The tasks to be done.
I shall walk on the cool green hills awhile
In the wind and the sun.
I shall stand on the heights and face the sky,
I shall breathe the air
That is clean and sweet; I shall lift my heart
In earnest prayer,
And all the problems that I have tried
To solve in vain
Will become crystal-clear, and the way
Will be made plain.
Then I shall go back to the waiting tasks,
But shall carry with me
The strength of God's hills and a beautiful new
Serenity.

In Thy Hand

IT COMFORTS me, O blessed Lord, recalling
  Thy gracious words: "My times are in thy hand!"
So often they have steadied me from falling,
So often in my journeying down the land
When briars clung and rough stones bruised my feet
I have found those dear words comforting and sweet.
"My times are in thy hand!" Help me remember
That nothing can separate me from my Lord;
It warms me like the glowing of an ember;
It strengthens me . . . I say it word by word,
Then face my day with courage and with hope
Enabled thus to climb earth's steepest slope.
"My times are in thy hand!" Why should I fear
Or falter with thy presence, Lord, so near?

Prayer for a Wider Vision

I BELONG to thee, O gracious loving Lord,
I am a child of thine with a heart on fire
For a wider vision than I yet have had:
That with these eyes I may see farther, higher
Into the vast unknown. Oh, may I view
Back of all beauty thy skilled hand, and trace
Thy voice upon the wind, and ever see
Within the dawn and sunset thy dear face.

Although life's storms may make my way seem dark
I shall not fear, nor falter, nor despair.
With steadfast eyes I shall behold the truth
That thou art in the midst, that thou art there.
Enlarge my vision, Lord, that I may see
Thy will is ever right and best for me.

In Quietness

> In quietness and in confidence shall be your strength.
>
> ISAIAH 30:15

WE CANNOT find God in the noisy throng;
    Where there are many voices, his is lost.
We lose our contact with him, and we wrong
His great outgiving heart, and at what cost!
"If we are quiet, help will come." The old
Folk song sounds out from a far land,
And in the words a vital truth is told.
Oh, may we listen, may we understand
That there are mountainsides we need to seek
Far from the jostling crowd, that we may hear
Within the sudden stillness God's voice speak,
And feel his blessed presence drawing near.
Only in quietness can we find strength
To live our best through any hour's length.

The Impregnable Rock

WHO stands upon it finds his footing sure:
A deep foundation though the storms run high,
A firm unshaken rock that will endure
Throughout eternity . . . Oh, lift the cry
That men may find this anchored rock and climb
To safety from the tempest of our time.

We read: "The word of God shall last forever,"
"Heaven and earth shall pass, but not my word,"
"The word of God is powerful. . . ." Oh, never
Has anything been surer! Blessed Lord,
We stand upon thy rock and no wild sea
Can tear us from this mooring built by thee.

Immortality

HE WHO doubts life's immortality,
  Who sees no future radiant and sublime,
Must stare with lusterless, dim eyes and see
The darkest sweep of wasteland of all time.
And sadder yet, the waste of life begun
And quickly spent, with but the briefest start
Toward knowledge—then before the day is done,
The sudden ceasing of the beating heart.

God will not have it so—there is no waste
Within his plan for man. He means we should
Go forward steadily, no undue haste
To mar a progress outlined for our good.
Each precious life he bids move upward, on,
Into a vaster realm than this, that we
May someday in Eternity's clear dawn
Find life, and live it more abundantly.

Altar Within the Heart

I HAVE reared an altar firmly within my heart,
A sacred place where I can go apart
And meet my Lord. At every day's bright start
I come to him, and find him waiting there.
Perhaps I come bowed down beneath some care,
Or burdened with a grief too great to bear,
And lo, he lifts the burden, shares the grief—
I know a sudden swift and sure relief,
And am strengthened for my days beyond belief.
It may be that I come at set of sun,
Glad to know my work has been well done,
Or with some spiritual victory I have won;
And behold, a love—wide as the sea is wide—
Awaits for me there at my altar's side,
Where my Lord abides, and ever will abide.

Chariots of Fire

> And the Lord opened the eyes of the young man; and he saw: and, behold, the mountain was full of horses and chariots of fire.
>
> II KINGS 6:17

ABOUT each child of God there stands unseen
A mountain filled with chariots of fire,
And no fierce enemy can forge between
Him and that clear flame lifting ever higher,
Lit by the hand of God thus to surround
The journeying pilgrims who are heavenward-
 bound.

"Fear not; for they that be with us are much more
Than they that be with them," the Prophet said.
Our unseen ally with its mighty store
Of power moves to conquer. . . . They have fled
Who sought our lives through greed and vain
 desire,
Curbed by invisible chariots of fire.

Have courage, hearts, fear not, be much in prayer;
The horses and the chariots are there.

A Universal Language

A CRY in need is a universal word
    Uttered by mankind. That cry is heard
By the living God, when it is fervent prayer.
He hears, he heeds, he answers. Why despair,
O troubled hearts, although the shadows grow
Deep as the night, and the tangled way we go
Seems dark and strange before our holden eyes?
God's ears are ever open to our cries.
His love is ours, his arm will be our stay,
He will bring us to the dawn of a new day
If we but wait his will. No race, no creed
Will be denied that comes to him in need.
He speaks, he understands, he has a part
In the universal language of the heart.

A Prayer for the Waking Ones

LORD, they are weary, and the night is long
    For these, the restless ones, who lie awake
Distressed and troubled by some inner wrong,
Or hurt and anxious for some loved one's sake.
It is for these tonight, O Lord, I pray.
Reach down thy gentle hand and bid them keep
As quiet as the stars that take their way,
And give them thy great healing gift of sleep.
A gift, indeed, thy priceless gift, dear Lord,
Provided for thy children! Let them find
This "treasure of the darkness" as reward
For tortured body and for troubled mind.
Lord God, I pray, bid pain and tension cease,
And give all sleepless ones thy blessed peace.

The Old Simplicities

THE heart with its ancient hunger seeks today
　　Among the fields for sustenance and finds
No grain to glean along the barren way,
No corn left in the husks, no mill that grinds.
The substitutes for food are poor, indeed,
To meet the spirit's and the body's need.

We are hungry for the old simplicities:
For the friendliness on which our parents fed,
For the long unhurried hours of quiet peace,
For neighborliness that was their daily bread,
For sympathy welling up at some heart's brink,
And for wayside pools of love at which to drink.

God, let us find among the husks, somewhere,
The old simplicities that should be there.

Because of His Compassion

BECAUSE of his compassion for his kind,
   He lives who never would be known at all
Had he not stopped his journeying to find
The roadside sufferer, who was too weak to call
Aloud for help and pity. Mercy shown,
And noticed by our Lord, has brought him fame,
Although through centuries no one has known
Where was his dwelling-place and what his name.

"A certain Samaritan," enough is told
In three brief words to bring a scene to view
Of beautiful compassion on the old,
Old road to Jericho. . . . God, may we too
Become immortal through some shining deed
Rendered to meet today's great human need!

Summer Evening

THE flaming light drains from the western sky;
  Soft-footed comes the dusk on field and hill,
And from a leafy hedgerow sound the shy
Notes of a hidden thrush. A cricket's shrill
Clamor rends the air, and down a lane
A boy shouts to another through the dusk.
The dew that falls is moist as gentle rain;
The wild flowers are as odorous as musk.

And suddenly across the dew-wet grass
And over the long hedgerows there is light
Where the lightning-laden fireflies flit and pass,
Signaling one another through the night.
And gleaming like a jewel, from afar
God sends his loveliest gift—the evening star.

Precious Fruit

THE man who plans an orchard plants his seedlings
Deep in the cool dark earth—then bides his time,
Waiting for the stir of roots, the sapling
To take its upward and unhindered climb,
Waiting for the bough, the bud, the blossom,
Waiting through the rain or bitter drought
For the perfect ripened globes of crimson brightness
That will be sweet as honey to his mouth.

Perhaps—who knows? the lengthened time of waiting
Within the dark for light to break may bring
To any troubled one eternal fruitage
That God withholds awhile—an offering
That will be sweeter to the taste for waiting,
That will be brighter when the dark is past—
O hearts, await his seasons, his rewarding,
The tree will bear its precious fruit at last.

A Holy Curiosity

"SEEK and ye shall find," the Master said;
   Much undiscovered riches lies ahead:
The soil still holds a further healing power,
The dock is near the nettle—any hour
The earnest prayerful seeking one may find
Some new resource to benefit mankind.
There is music yet to write that will inspire
The dullest heart—there are words that will set fire
To others when great poets pen their lines.
There will be generated light that shines
From unearthed metals, and new warmth to glow
From sources which as yet we do not know.
But for these sincere seekers on earth's sod
The greatest of all discoveries is God.

Preference

I WOULD not take the highroad to great power
Nor climb the dazzling mountain peaks to fame,
Lest, roughshod, I crush some frail wayside flower,
Or, sun-blind, fail to note the way I came.

I would not pay the price for adulation,
If through it I grew arrogant and proud;
For rather would I occupy some station
Where I might touch the lonely in the crowd;

Where I might say a word to ease some sorrow,
Or cheer some heart discouraged with its load,
Or share my store with those who come to borrow,
Or give my strength to lift another's load.

Thus would I live, thus would I die, forgetting
The sunlit heights of wealth and power and fame,
Content to go my way without regretting
If someone I have helped recalls my name.

I Shall Go On

There have been days of anguish, nights of pain,
The heart has ached, the way has not been clear;
But I shall take life by the hand once more
And by God's grace I shall go on from here.
Though I must journey for awhile alone
Since the hand I held in mine has loosed its hold,
I shall go on a way I have not known
Through summer's heat and through the winter's cold.

But an unseen Presence will be there to stay
My stumbling feet and give me power to stand.
I shall have his promised strength for every day,
As I move out across an untrod land.
I shall not falter and I shall not fear.
God helping me, I shall go on from here.

Out of the Ivory Palaces

OUT of the Ivory Palaces he came:
    Jesus, our Lord, into the world, so poor
That his only fire was a star's cold flame,
His only welcome was an Inn's closed door.
He came, the royal Heir of Heaven's Own,
To become the Son of man that we might be
The sons of God. He trod the earth alone
That we might proudly walk with royalty.

All hail the white incomparable Christ!
All hail the holy One, the sinless Lord!
The swiftly moving years have not sufficed
To give mankind the precious jeweled word
That will express the honor that we owe
To the humble Christ born centuries ago.

Hark! Across the World

HARK! across the world there is a singing
   Mingled with the silver sound of bells;
Voices lifting, and the high bells ringing,
And this the message that their music spells:
"The Christ is risen!" Hope bursts like a flower
Across the darkness of a lengthened night;
O hearts, lift up, be glad for this good hour
That brightens all Eternity with light.

Out of the shadow of an eastern garden
A form is moving, straight and tall and fair;
Death could not hold him, and the hired warden
Of soldiers had no power to stay him there.
O earth, rejoice, O mankind cease your weeping:
He has the power to meet our every need;
He holds the key of Heaven in his keeping;
The Christ is risen, he is risen, indeed.

About the Author

Born and raised in Indiana, Barry Wilson now lives and works in the midst of the Rocky Mountains. He is a twenty-six year veteran firefighter paramedic, currently working as a fire captain.

Barry spent seven of those years working part-time as a helicopter flight paramedic out of Page, Arizona on the shores of Lake Powell. There he worked rescues on Lake Powell, Grand Canyon, the Navajo Nation, and all of the surrounding areas.

After all those years of doing it, he is now ready to just sit back and write about it.

Bravo! I recommend it to everyone...a 10 out of 10.
—Conan Tigard, BookBrowser

As Engine Five turned onto Hempstead Drive, the fire crew could see the header of thick, black smoke billowing up from the middle of the block.

Engineer Graham yelled over the noise of the siren. "Looks like a burner, Cap!"

"Right on," Captain Evans said. "Looks like we're first in, too. Better find out if there's anyone still—"

The captain was interrupted by radio traffic.

Dispatch: "Engine Five and Engine Three. Reporting party states there are three children still in the structure, break...

Fires of Time

Fictional character Scott McLean, a fifth generation firefighter, gains the ability to travel back in time to relive some of American history's greatest fires. Can he stand by and watch the destruction, or will he save lives and change history?

"Barry Wilson's extensive fire service history shines through in his vivid portrayal of the men and women that serve daily in the streets. Being a female firefighter, the interpersonal relationships between Scott and his crew were especially appealing to me."
—Debby Honeycutt, firefighter paramedic

"*Fires of Time* is an epic journey that anyone who has ever answered the call, or wanted to, must take!"
—Raymond Anderson, firefighter paramedic

Visit us on the Web: $7.99 US
www.firesoftime.net $9.99 Can